I0803165

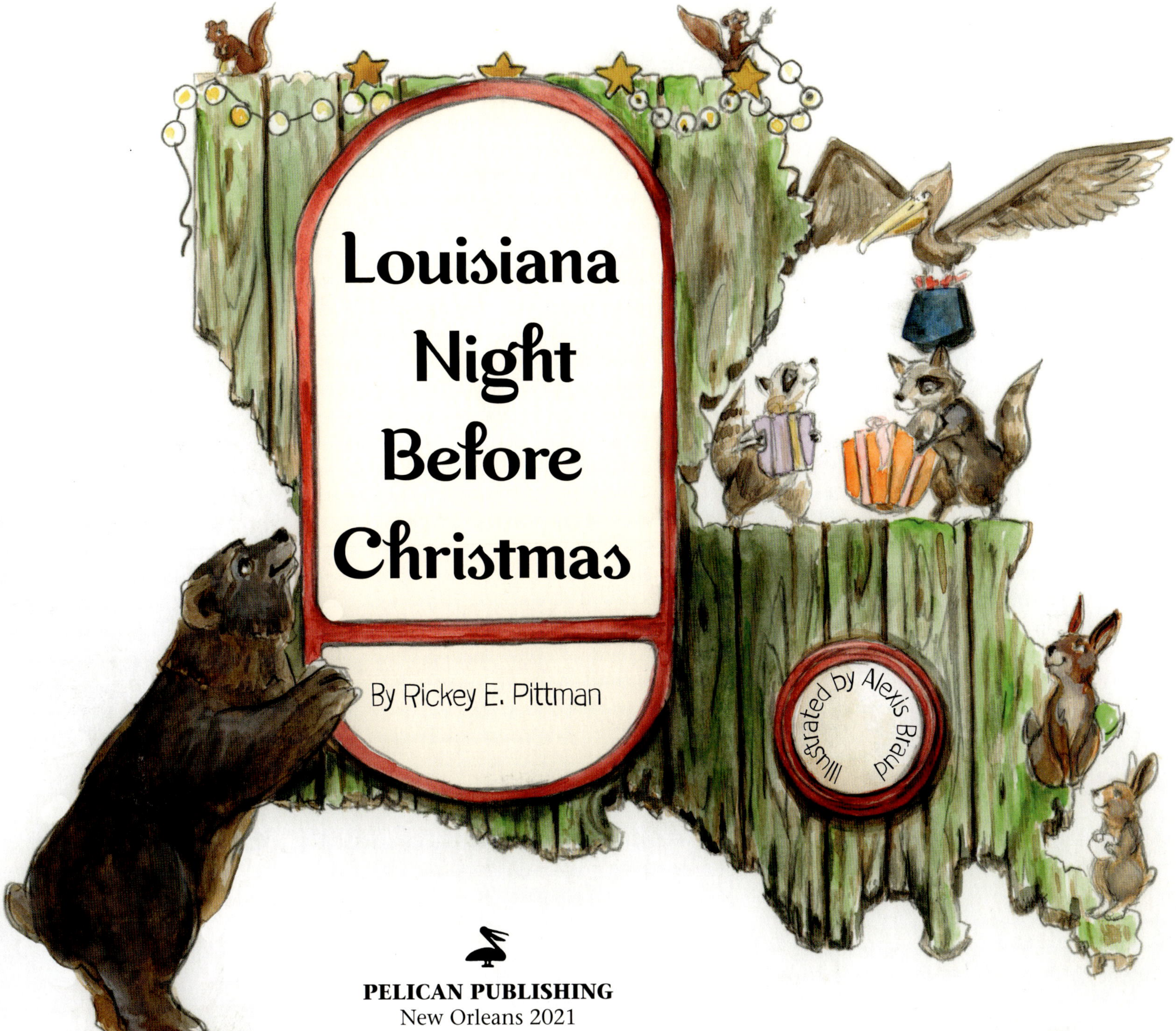

PELICAN PUBLISHING
New Orleans 2021

ISBN 9781455626601
Ebook ISBN 9781455626618

First River Road Press printing, 2020
First Pelican printing, 2021

Printed in Korea
Published by Pelican Publishing
New Orleans, LA
www.pelicanpub.com

To all the children of Louisiana.
And to the young at heart.

To my mother, Jessie Fae Pittman,
who always made Christmas special for her children.—REP

For Flo and Joe,
Merry Christmas.—AB

Papa Noël, he lives deep in the marsh,
Where critters are friendly
and skeeters are harsh.

But now the bayou is fraught
with doubt and fear,
For Christmas might not
even happen this year!

Papa Noël, he slipped on some moss.
He hit his ol' head and forgot he was boss.

He lay dere awhile and he stared at de sky.
He looked left, he looked right, and he said, "Who am I?"

He looked down at his boots,
but he was still dazed.
His backside was sore,
and his eyes was all glazed!

An elf come on by
and knew dis wasn't right!
He showed Papa to Mama
and she got her a fright.

She looked him all over and put him to bed.
She gave him some whiskey and ice for his head.

Papa, he say, "I don't know who I am.
All I remember is my head, it went BAM!"

She say, "Little elf, you done right
to get him back home.
If he'd stayed by da bayou,
he'd a-started to roam."

Mama said, “Now gather them elves
and dem animals too.
We gotta save Christmas
and that is fo’ true!”

Mama sprung into action
and lined up her troops;
The rabbits was working
to make hula hoops.

All day they was scurryin',
the big and the small;
Dey gotta save Christmas
for one and for all.

While the animals were busy
finishin' dem toys,
Da Catahoulas got fussed at
for makin' dey noise.

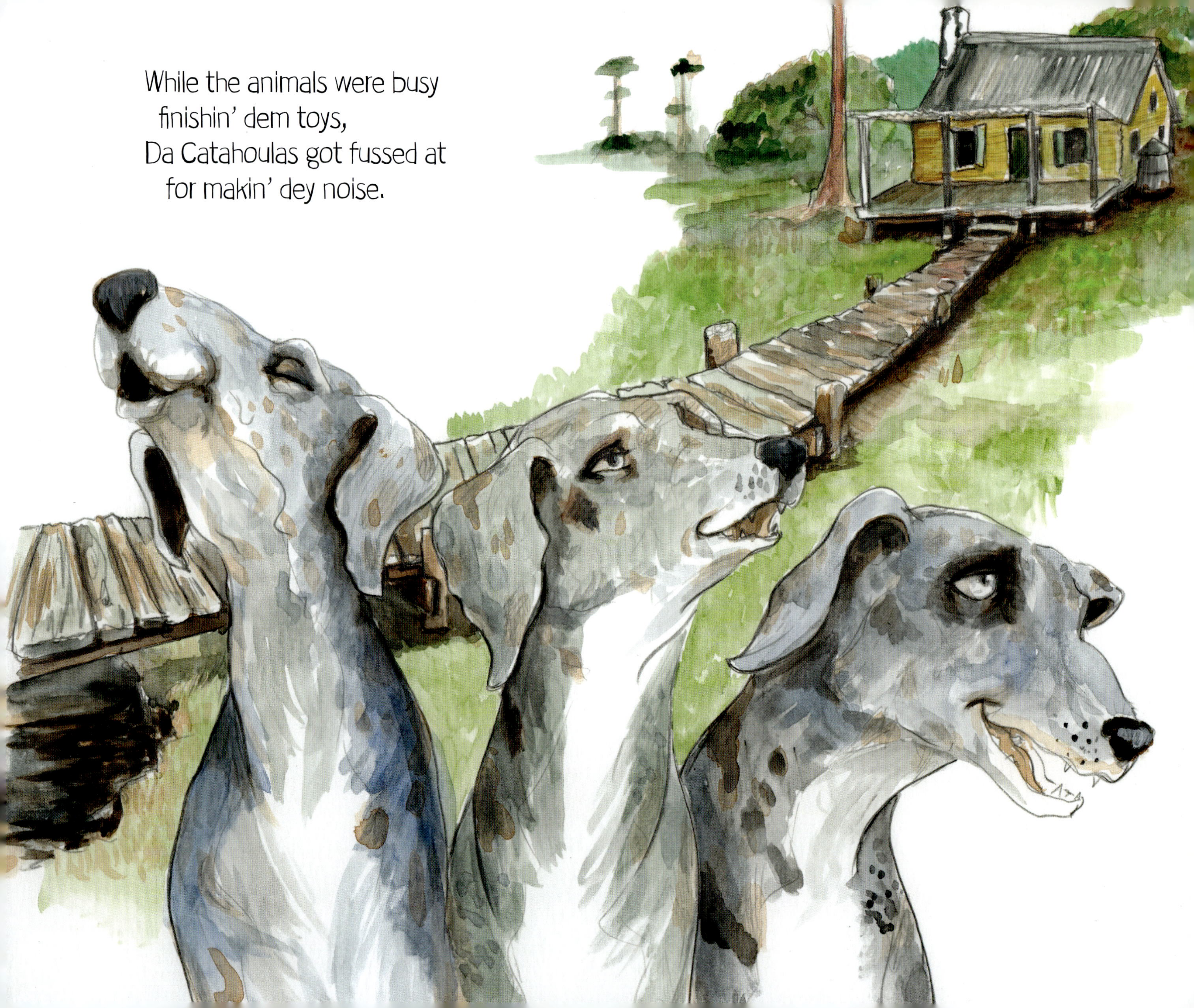

Raccoon said, "Here, take these dolls
and go straight to the sleigh!"
Then he tripped on a possum
who got in his way.

Dey was checkin' da list for
who's naughty or nice
When a nutria stepped up
to give some advice.

Mama say to dem animals,
"Y'all pack up dat sleigh.
We can't fool around;
we must not delay."

When the reindeer said,
"The sleigh's ready to go,"
The pelicans got scolded
for moving too slow!

Off dey went, off dey flew,
To Abbeville, Amite, and Arabi too.

On to Baldwin and Baker, Bastrop, and Boyce:
"You can't miss a spot, you ain't got a choice."

To Cameron, to Crowley, to Cut Off, and Scott:
"We ain't messin' up, we got just one shot!"

To Des Allemands, Empire, Eunice, and Gray:
"Y'all can't get tired. Keep pullin' this sleigh."

On to Gueydan and Gretna, Homer and Iota:
"Hit every house. We makin' that quota."

Now to Jena and Kenner, Lafayette and Larose:
"No time for a photo, not even a pose!"

Off to Lockport, Leesville, Mamou, and Monroe:
"We gotta keep goin' and finish dis show."

To Norco, New Orleans, Ponchatoula, and Rayne:
"We all just so tired, we might go insane."

Then to St. Gabriel, Tallulah, and Zachary:
Mama said, "We 'bout done now;
it's time for a daiquiri!"

Dey passed over the Superdome,
the Cajun Dome too;
Dey flew by Tiger Mike's home
and even saw Drew!

Kids everywhere,
they left out a treat,
Some of dem savory
and others quite sweet.

Hot chocolate, gumbo,
and pecan pralines.
One kid even made
a plate of red beans!

And dat's how it went, the long Christmas Eve night,
Till Papa lifted his head at morning's first light.

Mama told Papa just what dey had done;
Dey really worked hard, dey really had fun!

All found dere way home,
tired as could be;
Papa said, "Man,
y'all a real sight to see!"

"All y'all worked
through the rain and the cold
To save Christmas night
and reach every household!"

"We did it for you and the kids in the towns;
We didn't miss one, we made all the rounds.

"We all saved Christmas by working together,
Using every paw, wing, fin, flipper, and feather!

"Now don't ever get sick again, Papa Noël,"
The animals said as they bid him farewell.

"Merry Christmas, y'all!" he said with a grin,
"Until next December, when we do it again!"